Wild
NEW ENGLAND

A Celebration of Our Region's Natural Beauty

Stephen Gorman

Voyageur Press

First published in 2006 by Voyageur Press, an imprint of MBI Publishing Company, Galtier Plaza, Suite 200, 380 Jackson Street, St. Paul, MN 55101-3885 USA

MBI Publishing Company titles are also available at discounts in bulk quantity for industrial or sales-promotional use. For details write to Special Sales Manager at MBI Publishing Company, Galtier Plaza, Suite 200, 380 Jackson Street, St. Paul, MN 55101-3885 USA

Editor: Josh Leventhal
Designer: Liz Tufte

Printed in China

Library of Congress Cataloging-in-Publication Data

Gorman, Stephen.
  Wild New England : a celebration of our region's natural beauty / Stephen Gorman.
    p. cm.
  Includes bibliographical references and index.
  ISBN-13: 978-0-7603-2637-4
  ISBN-10: 0-7603-2637-1
  1. New England--Pictorial works. 2. New England--Description and travel. 3. Natural history--New England. 4. Natural history--New England--Pictorial works. 5. Landscape--New England--Pictorial works. 6. Natural areas--New England--Pictorial works. 7. Wilderness areas--New England--Pictorial works. I. Title.
  F5.G67 2006
  974.0022'2--dc22
                    2006003701

On the front cover: New Hampshire's White Mountain National Forest in early autumn.

On the back cover (clockwise from upper left): Acadia National Park, Maine; near the Appalachian Trail, Vermont; Kent Falls State Park, Connecticut; Cape Cod National Seashore, Massachusetts.

Page 1: Beach grasses grow at the edge of the dunes at Cape Cod National Seashore in Massachusetts.

Page 2: Mount Chocorua and the Sandwich Range Wilderness are reflected in the waters of Chocorua Lake, White Mountain National Forest.

Page 3: A paper birch stands beside the Appalachian Trail in Vermont amidst a hardwood stand in autumn.

Page 4: Snowy birches line a mountain stream on a December morning in Maine's Mahoosuc Range.

Page 5: The sheer cliffs of Mount Kineo rise above the waters of Moosehead Lake in the Maine Woods.

Page 6: The stormy sea pounds the rocky shoreline of Acadia National Park at Otter Cliffs.

Page 7: The frosty peaks of New Hampshire's Kilkenny Ridge rise above the snow-covered Israel River.

Page 8: A wave strikes and recedes below Otter Cliffs.

Page 9: A makeshift footbridge crosses Wadleigh Stream deep in the Maine Woods.

Title page, main image: Alpenglow strikes the summit of Borestone Mountain high above Onawa Lake in the Maine Woods.

Title page, inset: Autumn leaves dot a rivulet along the Appalachian Trail in Vermont's Upper Connecticut River Valley.

On the facing page: A curious cow moose pauses while wading in the Moose River of Maine.

DEDICATION

To Mary Borah Gorman, for her amazing support and encouragement;
and to Tasha, for simply being the best dog ever, period.

ACKNOWLEDGMENTS

It has been a pleasure to work on this volume with Josh Leventhal of Voyageur Press. Most of the time, collaborating over vast distances by phone and e-mail can be difficult, but that has not been the case this time around.

I also would like to thank the generous people of the Upper Valley of Vermont and New Hampshire for all the friendship, support, and encouragement they have shown me; and also for their collective commitment to living in harmony with their beautiful surroundings. They set an example the rest of the nation might emulate.

Contents

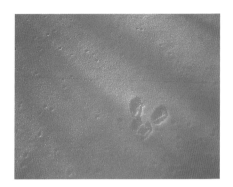

INTRODUCTION

Above
A boulder sticks out at a jaunty angle from the calm
surface of Maine's Upper Richardson Lake.

Left
Rivers, forests, and mountains. New England's dramatic
and varied landscape is evident along this stretch of the
Penobscot River on a late autumn day.

T O THOSE FROM "AWAY" (as old-time Yankees refer to the rest of the world) the words "New England" conjure an incredible variety of contrasting images.

For many people, New England represents the flowering of great American cultural institutions, American industry, American liberty, and American literature. For others, New England evokes thoughts of lighthouses, white-steeple churches, weathered barns, covered bridges, and fiery autumn hillsides. For some, New England represents the pinnacle of American higher education, or American shipbuilding, or the American fishing industry; while for others it is a region of thriving cities home to cutting-edge technology firms.

When some people think of New England, they see the cobbled streets of Beacon Hill in Boston, while others think of the rugged Maine coast and lobsters. For still others, however, New England means the empty sands and sweeping dunes of Cape Cod. Or a wilderness of mountains, forests, rivers, and lakes.

Of course, New England is all of these things and much, much more.

On the bold coast of Maine, harbor seals bask in the sunshine on rockbound islands. In the Maine Woods, moose feed in wild rivers and lakes. In the high White Mountains, arctic tundra plants cling to slopes and outcrops. In the sandy barren plains of Cape Cod, vigilant hikers watch out for the sharp spines of prickly pear cactus. (Cactus? In New England? Yes, along with balsam fir and sugar maple, prickly pear is a native plant.) Off the shores of Monomoy, Cuttyhunk, and Block Island, great white sharks scavenge humpback-whale carcasses and hunt gray seals.

Less than one-third the size of California, and just a measly two percent of the total land area of the United States, the compact New England nonetheless feels as if it must actually be incredibly large—how can such a small area possibly contain so many different natural and human environments? After all, it is home to one of the continent's major mountain ranges and numerous lesser ranges, vast forests, twelve major river basins, sandy terminal moraines such as Cape Cod, Nantucket, and Martha's Vineyard, and more than six thousand miles of ocean coastline sprinkled with more than four thousand islands. (Off the Maine coast alone there are more islands than in all of the Caribbean and in all of Polynesia!)

Look at a relief map of New England, or better yet, run the palm of your hand over one. Feel the bumps, ridges, and gaps—hills and mountains and valleys. It's an ancient, gnarled, twisted, contorted surface—uplifted, folded, and faulted by tremendous forces beneath the earth, built of molten rock spewed from miles underground—whose only smooth sections are those immediately along some sections of the coastline of Massachusetts and Rhode Island. In Vermont, where I live, there's a saying that if you could figure out a way to steam iron Vermont flat like a shirt and smooth all the wrinkles, it would be bigger than Texas. True or not, in the Green Mountain State you are either going up, or you are going down.

Above
The woods of the Vermont mountains take on a striking and mysterious aura in winter.

Facing page
A rocky outcrop juts into the turbulent waters of the North Atlantic Ocean at the base of Otter Cliffs in Acadia National Park.

The snow-capped Mount Washington, New England's highest peak, rises above the Mount Washington Valley on a clear morning in May.

Though New England has been settled by Europeans for a very long time—Boston is older than St. Petersburg, Russia—much of the region qualifies as some of the wildest, least-visited land in the United States. Though York, on the Maine coast, is the country's oldest incorporated town—established by English settlers in 1624—the interior of Maine wasn't officially explored for another two hundred years, around the same time that Lewis and Clark were investigating the Louisiana Purchase thousands of miles to the west.

It wasn't a lack of curiosity that kept English settlers from venturing more than a few miles inland; it was mortal terror. The English were pinned to the New England coastline and offshore islands for a couple of hundred years by the horror inflicted upon them by French and Indian raiding parties. Virtually all of northern New England was a brutal killing ground where any foolish attempt at settlement would have been swiftly wiped out.

That fear of violent death, along with the implacable nature of the landscape and climate, set the settlement pattern for many generations. Even today much of the interior is sparsely populated, and indeed the Maine Woods includes the largest uninhabited region in all of the lower forty-eight states, a fact that might surprise people from "Away."

The great Western writer Wallace Stegner once called New England "a rugged land with a violent climate." He knew what he was talking about, for the Pulitzer Prize– and National Book Award–winning author spent a good deal of his time writing about the West while at his camp in Vermont's wild Northeast Kingdom. He fed the woodstove and cranked out his novels and essays while the thermometer dropped to forty-five below zero and blizzards howled outside his window.

Make no mistake; this is truly a rugged land with violent weather. Northern New England has a climate similar to that of south-central Alaska, which is a thousand miles farther north. As I write this in mid-October, there are twelve-foot snowdrifts and hurricane-force winds atop New Hampshire's Mount Washington.

It may come as a surprise to some that Concord, in southern New Hampshire, has a lower record-low temperature and higher record snowfall than Anchorage, Alaska; and that Boston, Massachusetts, averages more snow annually than Minneapolis, Minnesota. (Boston is also the country's windiest city, claims by Chicago and San Francisco notwithstanding.) Jay Peak in Vermont receives more snow annually (355 inches, or about 30 feet) than Aspen or Vail in Colorado.

In part because of this meteorological hostility—Yankees have a saying that goes, "We have nine months of winter and three months of damned poor sledding"— people have continued to stay away from large portions of New England in droves,

A remnant from the area's earlier farmland existence, an old stone wall runs through the forest near Sandwich Notch, New Hampshire.

Autumn may be New England's finest
season, as exhibited by this glorious
hillside in the Upper Connecticut
River Valley of Vermont.

opting instead for milder climes in the nation's Sunbelt. (Summer's onslaught of biting blackflies is another reason for those seeking comfort not to stick around.) My home state, Vermont, ranks forty-ninth in population, right behind Alaska and just ahead of Wyoming, which leaves a lot of wild, open, unpopulated spaces.

Because of the short growing season and the rugged, rocky contours, much of New England has never been easy to farm. When lands in the Midwest and West became available to settlers in the mid-1800s, people fled their New England hill farms. As a result of New England's mid-century diaspora, the vast majority of the land once cleared for frustrating attempts at farming was abandoned and has reverted back to forest. Indeed, it's not unusual to stumble across old cellar holes and bits of stone wall in deep, dark woods. The result of the mass exodus is that today New England is once again the most heavily forested region in the country.

Mountains. Forests. Rivers and lakes. Beaches. Rocky coastlines. Islands. All within a day's travel of one another. All constantly changing with the seasons. All relentlessly defying expectations.

So, do I have your interest? I hope so, because as you can probably tell, I am rather fond of this peculiar region. Like a shape-shifting shaman, New England presents a different face, a different form, each time you look. With such diversity of landscapes and with such variety and volatility of seasons, New England presents endless opportunities for exploration and adventure. I hope you enjoy this interpretation of the region presented through my words and images, and I also hope that they spur you to action—to see for yourself what's out there, and then to vigorously defend it by helping to keep it wild.

Rhode Island may be our nation's smallest state, but it has its share of stunning wilderness scenes. This freshwater lake is located in Burlingame State Park.

Chapter 1

THE ROCKBOUND COAST

ACADIA NATIONAL PARK

Above
Sunlight bathes the granite bedrock of Otter Cliffs in a rich, warm light on a summer morning in Acadia National Park.

Left
The rising sun strikes the coast of Maine, illuminating rounded beach cobbles and the sheer faces of Otter Cliffs in Acadia.

A N OFFSHORE BREEZE spilling down from high, rocky bluffs caressed my face as I stood at the portside rail of a sailing ship. I turned to watch the wind fill the expansive cream-colored sails. High over the water, atop each of three tall, wooden masts, the flags of the State of Maine, the United States, and the schooner snapped to attention in the cool autumn breeze.

As the canvas billowed and the heavy halyards stretched taut with a creaking sound, the green ship with white trim heeled ever so slightly to starboard. An unexpected rush of forward motion accompanied the wind as the 170-foot-long, 24-foot-wide, 208-ton vessel came to life and pitched forward through the cold, dark water. The ship was free at last from the windless doldrums that had kept her in irons for the better part of two days.

I felt a tremor of excitement on deck as the twenty-odd passengers, guests on a cruise along the rockbound coast and islands of Maine, put down their books and crossword puzzles and stood to the rails, peering out with renewed interest across the indigo waters of Penobscot Bay. Like the ship, they too seemed suddenly reanimated, as though they had merely been awaiting a fresh breeze to bring them back to life.

The ship breaking spiritedly through the froth, sending up sheets of salty spray from her bow, was the *Victory Chimes*, a three-masted schooner built of stout pine and oak in 1900. She was a rugged, graceful ship, with pleasing lines tapering to a jaunty upswept bow. Her bold carriage struck me as appropriate for a ship that started out in life as a member of that esteemed class of swift, sturdy cargo vessels called "ram" schooners—dependable ships designed to carry lumber up and down the Atlantic Coast.

Today, the *Victory Chimes* is the last of her generation, the only original three-masted schooner in the windjammer fleet, and a hard-working tribute to the Age of Sail. The largest passenger sailing ship flying the Stars and Stripes (the *Victory Chimes* can accommodate up to forty guests), she sails out of Rockland, Maine, a midcoast town whose residents have made their living for over two centuries by going down to the sea.

On the rockbound coast of Maine, the forested granite mountaintops, worn smooth by the glaciers of the last ice age, meet the sea.

We were cruising to Mount Desert Island and Acadia National Park, heading east across Penobscot Bay, when eight other tall schooners emerged from the protected harbors of Rockland and nearby Camden, raised their sails, and ventured out onto the bay in a scene recaptured from another era. Watching from the rails, a retired Navy man from Delaware said, "It's like we've sailed back in time."

Old Salts have hailed the bony, island-studded Maine coast as a sailor's paradise since the sixteenth century, when Giovanni Verrazano became the first known European to cruise these waters in 1524. The Italian explorer described the rockbound Maine coast as scattered with islands "all near the continent; small and

pleasant in appearance, but high; following the curve of the land; some beautiful ports and channels formed between them." He compared the Maine archipelago to the islands of the Adriatic, perhaps a fair comparison if climate is removed from the equation.

These myriad islands (no one knows the exact number, official tallies put the total at over three thousand) and abundant bays make the Maine coast arguably the best sailing ground in North America, offering limitless opportunities for interesting journeys in every direction. The remarkable shoreline bends, twists, and turns along the mainland and among the islands and bays for an astonishing 3,500 miles—all compressed into accordion-like folds between the border with New Hampshire to the southwest and New Brunswick to the northeast, a distance of a mere 250 miles as the crow flies.

The story of Acadia and the remarkable Maine coast began some five hundred million years ago, when molten rock miles beneath the earth's surface began squeezing up into cracks and fissures in the overlying strata. The irruption cooled partway to the surface, where it formed an enormous dome of pink granite. Over the next

Beach grasses grow from a pure white beach of pulverized sea shells—not sand—on one of Maine's many offshore islands.

two hundred million years, erosion wore away the surface layers atop the dome, eventually revealing an east–west granite ridge called the Mount Desert Range.

Then, about twenty thousand years ago during the last ice age, a massive ice sheet over a mile thick flowed down across the landscape of Maine. The ice scraped and gouged and tore at the rock, wreaking havoc and devastation until it rammed into the Mount Desert Range lying directly in its path.

There the glacier stalled, but not for long. The force of billions of tons of ice flowing down from Canada eventually broke the stalemate, and the glacier surged over the Mount Desert Range. Cutting and chiseling, the glacier raked the pink granite ridge. Then the glacier accelerated, cracking giant stone blocks from the mountain and carving the sheer cliffs along the oceanfront as it flowed down the face of the range toward the sea.

When the ice age ended some ten thousand years ago, the landscape left behind was drastically altered. The unbroken Mount Desert Range was carved into a series of north–south ridges separated by wide, U-shaped valleys. And as the ice sheet melted, some of the troughs and vales filled with water to become freshwater lakes and ponds. Giant boulders, called glacial erratics, were left strewn across the landscape. Some of these rocks ended up in improbable positions perched on the sides of mountains. Flooded with melt water, the sea rose dramatically. It flooded the continental shelf and drowned the inland valleys and hills, creating the meandering shoreline and myriad islands that characterize the Maine coast today.

The first seafarers to venture over the waters off of Acadia were the Abenaki, a native tribe who hunted, fished, and foraged here for thousands of years prior to European settlement. Using birch-bark canoes ranging in size from small, single-man models to huge vessels capable of carrying a ton or more, the Abenaki were familiar with all of Maine's islands, even those twenty miles out to sea.

The Abenaki traveled from their winter inland homes to the coast in summer to escape the ferocious mosquitoes and blackflies of the interior forests. They used the islands as summer encampments for hunting and fishing excursions, gathering molting waterfowl in the marshes; hunting seals, porpoises, and bluefin tuna offshore; harpooning whales in the deeper bays; plucking lobsters from the spiny reefs; and gathering clams, berries, and roots on the islands themselves.

The Native Americans were likely visited by mysterious strangers about a thousand years ago when serpentine long ships bearing bearded, pale-skinned men appeared out of the foggy Atlantic. Legend has it that the Vikings merely passed through the islands, stopping neither to trade nor plunder. Whatever the Norsemen found here on the rocky coast, it wasn't what they were looking for, and they were never seen again.

Rounded, glaciated mountains called the Bubbles rise above the south end of Eagle Lake in the interior of Mount Desert Island.

Six centuries later, French explorer Samuel de Champlain sailed along this wild. From his ship's deck he saw bold, rocky headlands crowned by thick forests of spruce and fir. Off the coast he saw gleaming granite islands breaching from the cold, dark depths, some of them rising a thousand feet above the sea, while others merely broke the surface or were covered when the tide was high.

Landing on one of the larger islands, Champlain was impressed by the smooth, sloping mountains, and he called it *L'isle des Monts Deserts,* "the island of the bare mountains." (The Abenaki already had a name for the island, calling it *Pemetic,* "the sloping land.") And then he named another island off to the west *L'isle au Haut,* "the high island," for the spectacular way it thrust high above the sea.

Much of Maine and its islands remained under French control until England secured victory in the French and Indian Wars in 1763 and brought the region within the British Empire. Settlement of Mount Desert Island proceeded gradually until the mid-1800s, when the spectacular paintings by artists such as Thomas Cole and Frederic Church exposed the beauty of the region to a wider audience. By the turn of the nineteenth century, it was a popular retreat for wealthy easterners, who also worked to help preserve the landscapes.

In 1916, President Wilson proclaimed the establishment of Sieur de Monts National Monument, encompassing Mount Desert Island, Isle au Haut, and the

Early morning fog creeps in over the edge of a rockbound island in the Deer Isle Thoroughfare.

Schoodic Peninsula. Three years later, Wilson signed the act establishing it as the first national park east of the Mississippi, calling it Lafayette National Park. The name was changed to Acadia National Park in 1929.

Today Acadia National Park offers some of the best and most diverse outdoor recreation of any park in the country. Over one hundred miles of maintained and marked trails provide a truly unique network of mountain, forest, lakeshore, and ocean paths. The trails run the gamut from easy beach walking to strenuous, all-day affairs up precipitous cliffs and over the bare, pink-granite summits. Sometimes thick ocean fog limits visibility on the granite summits to only a few feet, but on clear days, trails such as the Western Head Trail on Isle au Haut offer spectacular views of the sea from high oceanside cliffs.

In the early years of the twentieth century, John D. Rockefeller, an early park benefactor, built a system of carriage paths on Mount Desert Island that he placed off-limits to automobile travel. Rockefeller considered automobiles "infernal machines," and he felt the narrow, winding gravel paths provided a way to enjoy the magnificent scenery of Acadia without compromising the environment. Now restored, Rockefeller's legacy consists of a fifty-seven-mile network of tracks winding throughout the eastern side of the island. Still barred to automobiles, the paths are perfect for walking, skiing, horseback riding, and, of course, mountain biking. They are a terrific way to explore the incredible natural diversity of the park and to enjoy the ocean views, interior lakes, forests, mountains, and waterfalls.

Though sailors have been exploring Acadia's rocky, island-studded coast since Verrazano, today the pleasures of coasting are no longer restricted to the yacht-club set. More and more people are discovering that the sea kayak is perhaps the vessel best suited for exploring all of these bays, harbors, islands, coves, and inlets. A kayaker can circumnavigate Mount Desert Island or paddle out to the Porcupine Islands in Bar Harbor; explore the deep reaches of Somes Sound; or pack a lunch and paddle out to some deserted island in Merchant Row off Stonington to haul out with the seals on a smooth granite shelf, watch the lobster boats ply their trade, and catch a few winks in the sunshine.

Winter can be a spectacular time to visit Acadia as well. The season often brings clear, sharp days with excellent views of the mountains and the ocean; and with normally ample snowfall in the park, skiing in Acadia can be magnificent. A real treat is cruising the expansive snowfields atop the bare granite summits with the open ocean below, or touring the park's many miles of carriage paths.

Back on the *Victory Chimes* it is midday, and the fog that had settled in during the night has burned off. This being our last day aboard ship, we are pointed back to Rockland, north and west across the heart of Penobscot Bay.

Looking across the cold North Atlantic towards Isle au Haut, "the high island," so named by French explorer Samuel de Champlain in the early 1600s.

Exiting the Deer Isle Thoroughfare, a navigational passage between Deer Isle to the north and a large group of smaller islands to the south, we watch harbor seals watching us as we pass their sunny haul-out ledges. At the entrance to the bay, a pod of porpoises swims lazily about a hundred yards away, the crescent shapes of their arched backs and dorsals rising and falling with a graceful rhythm.

Suddenly the wind picks up. It flows like water from the land down the slopes of Blue Hill and Cape Rozier. I make my way to the stern, where Captain Paul DeGaeta stands at the wheel, a broad grin creasing his dark-tanned face.

The captain urges me to take a turn at the helm. I happily oblige and take my place behind the spoked, polished wooden wheel. Bright pennants snap in the breeze and I alternately glance up at the sails or down at the compass and charts. As I experiment with the controls, the leviathan ship lumbers heavily through the water, the embodiment of inexorable force. Within moments of taking the helm, I understand why sailors refer to their ships as pronouns, for this vessel certainly seems to have a mind and personality of her own.

Alone at the wheel of a wooden sailing ship, cruising through a still-pristine environment little changed by humans, I find it easy to slip back in time and imagine what early European adventurers saw as they searched this mysterious coastline.

After a while I relinquish the wheel to the captain. At dinner the night before he had called the ship a "museum under sail." Looking off across the sparkling water toward Isle au Haut I feel he sold the vessel short, for she is much more than a floating exhibit of the musty past. Sailing Acadia and the rockbound coast of Maine is a chance to step back in time, if only for a few days, and relive the adventures of those who have gone before us.

A powerful wave crashes into the south coast of Mount Desert Island during hurricane season in September. These waves can hurl large beach cobbles far inland, and have swept many unsuspecting park visitors out to sea.

Left
At the edge of the North Atlantic, the Otter Cliffs highlight the varied and dramatic beauty of Acadia National Park.

Above
A cleft in the rocks at Otter Cliffs offers a view of the crashing sea into the shores of Acadia.

Sunrise illuminates the rockbound shores of an island in the Deer Isle Thoroughfare off the coast of Maine.

The warm summer sun can barely penetrate a thick sea fog rising from the frigid waters of the Gulf of Maine in the Deer Isle Thoroughfare.

On the flanks of Cadillac Mountain in Acadia National Park, long glacial striations scar the pink granite bedrock.

The placidity of the many freshwater lakes and ponds on the Mount Desert Island interior defies the turmoil of its rocky coast. Lake Wood, shown here, is just inland of the island's visitor center.

The Bubbles frame the northern end of Jordan Pond in the interior of Mount Desert Island.

The sheer cliffs of Beech Mountain rise above the still blue waters of Echo Lake in the interior of Mount Desert Island, Acadia National Park.

The freshwaters of Bass Harbor Marsh flow from the western mountains of Mount Desert Island to the Atlantic Ocean at sunset.

The bold coastline of Maine glows in the first light of day.

The angry North Atlantic continues to boil beneath the Otter Cliffs long after a storm has passed.

A large wave looms over the beach cobbles on the shore of Acadia National Park.

The forces of land and sea wage a battle for supremacy every day at Acadia National Park.

An angular boulder rests on an offshore island, where it was deposited by retreating glaciers at the end of the last ice age some ten thousand years ago.

The sun sets over the golden waters of Penobscot Bay on a summer evening.

Chapter 2

THE FOREST

BAXTER STATE PARK

Above
Beaver tooth marks scar the lower trunks of a birch tree in winter, near Zealand Pond in New Hampshire's White Mountains.

Left
Late-afternoon sunlight filters through the spruce and fir trees of the Maine Woods.

THE APPALACHIAN TRAIL snakes through the deep North Woods of Maine, winding between thick walls of hardwood and evergreen forests on its way to the East's most remarkable mountain: Katahdin. A wild, solitary peak—"rising from a vast forest plain, like an island from an illimitable ocean," as an early climber, William Larrabee, described it in the 1800s—Katahdin remained hidden behind the vast, unbroken forestlands for over a century and a half after European settlement of Maine's shores.

Today, the 5,267-foot Katahdin stands as the centerpiece of Baxter State Park, a 314-square-mile chunk of protected wilderness in the heart of Maine's fabled North Woods. The park itself is surrounded by ten million or so acres of unpopulated wildlands that encompass the largest uninhabited region in the continental United States.

The park's namesake, Percival P. Baxter, was an ardent conservationist who worked determinedly throughout his life to ensure that Katahdin and the surrounding forest would be protected from predatory logging practices. A true independent, as a young man Baxter was an original hippie. He was jailed at political rallies and called a "longhair" in the press. As he matured, he became a formidable political force and went on to serve as Governor of Maine from 1921 to 1925, becoming one of Maine's most popular governors.

A man of action, Baxter personally bought the mountain and the adjacent lands piece by piece from the forest-products companies who owned virtually the entire northern portion of the state. During the first three decades of the twentieth century, he purchased more than two hundred thousand acres of forest, and then transferred these lands to the people of Maine under the condition that they "shall be forever left in the wild natural state." In 1933, the state legislature, which had declined to contribute a single cent to the purchase, named the park in Baxter's honor. Perhaps no greater gift has ever been bequeathed to the people of a state.

The mile-high ramparts of Mount Katahdin emerge majestically from the dense forests of Baxter State Park.

"The works of men are short-lived," said Baxter. "Monuments decay, buildings crumble, wealth vanishes, but Katahdin and its massive grandeur will forever remain the mountain of the people of Maine."

A surveyor named Joseph Chadwick was the first European to see Katahdin. He came upon it in 1763 while surveying the Penobscot River watershed for the state of Massachusetts, which controlled Maine at the time. After that brief glimpse, however, the forest closed in again, cloaking Katahdin in mystery for another forty years. The great mountain was all but forgotten until it was rediscovered by the first official exploration of Maine's interior in 1804.

During my own exploration of Maine's forested interior, some two centuries later, I walk the wooded Appalachian Trail under brooding skies on a damp, chilly June evening. Since crossing the last logging road earlier that morning, I have put

Autumn leaves carpet the forest floor along the Appalachian Trail in the Green Mountains.

in a full day, hiking along the wild West Branch of the Penobscot River, crossing a vast area recovering from a forest fire in 1977, and stopping for a leisurely trail lunch by the limpid pools and thundering falls of Little Niagara. Currently, the daylight is fading and the footpath is rough, forcing me to pay attention and focus on my surroundings.

I savor such evenings in the fathomless dark forest. Resting for a moment, I sniff the fir-scented air, the fragrance of damp, rotting leaves and bark, and listen to the somber rain drip from feathery balsams. Off in the gloom, I hear a sharp crack, and a muffled thump lets me know I have company in these woods. A little farther on, a moose, head held high, emerges from the mysterious forest. He gazes at me solemnly for a moment, then gives his head a little toss and trots across the trail with a long-legged, ungainly dignity. The woods swallow him and in a few moments he vanishes.

Baxter State Park encompasses a rich diversity of terrain, from expansive woodlands, to rivers and lakes, to mountain peaks. And though quite popular in summer, much of it remains virtually unknown. Discoveries of natural features in the park's backcountry were being made as late as the 1930s. Even today, still hidden behind the barrier of the Great North Woods, vast sections of the preserve are trail-less and receive little, if any, use.

Because the hour is late and the weather raw, I am thankful I chose to spend my first night in Baxter at Daicey Pond, one of the many lakes gouged out of the landscape during the last ice age. Here a rustic cabin awaits, complete with bunk, gas lantern, and wood stove. Tonight I will live the ancient dream of the north: a rough-hewn cabin deep in the forest, a solitary self-sufficiency in the wildest country. I will feel the forest's clammy embrace, listen to the prehistoric cries of loons across the lake, and pretend, if only for a while, that this mythic existence is truly my own.

Countless streams and rivers flow through the forests of New England, including the boulder-filled Rocky Branch, tumbling down from New Hampshire's White Mountains in summer.

Snug and warm inside my cabin, lounging comfortably in a rocker and feeling fully relaxed, I hear the trees dripping outside in the falling dark. As the last faint light fades, the cold drizzle lets up, the curtain of leaden cloud slowly lifts, and Katahdin is revealed: a massive stone fortress etched against a mauve sky, looming high above the taiga and the mirrored surface of the pond.

Meaning "Greatest Mountain" in the language of the Penobscot Indians, Katahdin is a steep-sided, rugged massif gouged with glacial cirques and topped with vast alpine tablelands. Sharply serrated ridges stretch more than four miles from the summit of Baxter Peak, the mountain's apex. Remote and severe, Katahdin's massive front rises sharply 4,500 feet above the surrounding boreal forest; and it watches over a collection of lesser peaks, eighteen of which rise above 3,500 feet.

Early the next morning I hike through the Katahdin Stream campground and head for the summit on the Hunt Trail, which also happens to be the terminal section of the Appalachian Trail. Invigorated by the bracing air of this cool June morning, I dress warmly, adding hat and gloves to ward off the chill. At this hour no one else is up and about, so I start down the trail by myself, thinking of Henry David Thoreau—the bard of Walden, the village crank—who set out to climb this mountain in 1846 but was turned back short of the summit by the elements.

The Hunt Trail parallels Katahdin Stream, climbing moderately at first through a mixed hardwood forest, occasionally crossing an open area strewn with large boulders of the fine pink and white granite characteristic of the park. After about a mile, a side trail leads through the trees to reveal Katahdin Stream Falls, a striking fifty-foot cascade thundering out of the mist-shrouded spruce and fir.

New England is the most heavily forested region in the United States, and Maine is our most heavily forested state; New Hampshire is second, while Vermont ranks third. I have been told by foresters that if all the wood in New England were cut down and stacked in cords—four by four by eight feet—the resulting woodpile would circle the globe some forty times.

New England's heavy forest cover was not always here. Prior to European settlement the region was covered by mature primeval forest, but beginning in the 1600s farmers began clearing the land for agriculture. By the middle of the nineteenth century, crops and pastures covered nearly three-quarters of the arable land in southern and central New England. But after the Civil War much of the land was abandoned for richer farmland to the west, and forests again blanketed more than seventy-five percent of the region.

Today, New England hosts a rich mosaic of different forest types varying with latitude and elevation. In the three southern New England states, deciduous

On a frosty February morning, the Green River tumbles past the bare deciduous trees and lush evergreens in the Berkshire Hills of western Massachusetts.

trees such as the chestnut oak, scarlet oak, black oak, white oak, and red maple are residents of the hilltops. On the mid-slopes, black birch, white birch, shagbark hickory, and flowering dogwood are commonly found. The low-slope forest is home to red oak, white ash, and tupelo. On the sand plains of Cape Cod and the islands of Nantucket and Martha's Vineyard, the most common trees are pitch pine and bear oak.

In the valleys of the three northern New England states, northern hardwoods such as sugar maple, beech, and birch are common; lower mountain slopes are characterized by a mixture of red spruce, balsam fir, maple, beech, birch, white pine, and red pine; lastly, upper mountain slopes are home to pure stands of balsam fir and red spruce.

The forest in Baxter State Park is representative of northern New England, where the northern hardwood forest meets the boreal forest. Here in the North Woods, the sugar maple, beech, birch, and ash occupy the sites with deeper, better-drained soils, while the spruce and fir, so reminiscent of the Canadian north, prefer the cold hollows, meandering stream flats, and higher mountain slopes.

Thoreau, as usual, had a few comments about the New England forests. Writing in *The Maine Woods*, he said: "The hard woods, occasionally occurring exclusively, were less wild to my eye. I fancied them ornamental grounds, with farmhouses in the rear. . . . The evergreen woods had a decidedly sweet and bracing fragrance; the air was a sort of diet-drink, and we walked on buoyantly in Indian file, stretching our legs."

Watching the opaque veil swirl through the dark green boughs, cling briefly to them, then disappear, I eavesdrop on the falls and the wind gusting unseen overhead. After a few moments, I press on toward tree line. There, I will enter the desolate realm of Pamola, the winged, howling mountain-storm god of the Penobscot. Half man, half eagle, Pamola wields the power to destroy those who venture into his blustery domain.

The Hunt Trail exits the shelter of the stunted, weather-blasted conifers and ascends steeply up the sharply serrated ridge of the Hunt Spur. Now the climbing becomes scrambling through, over, and around giant granite boulders—"the raw materials of a planet dropped from an unseen quarry," as Thoreau described the mountain's flanks.

Wind tears at the clouds, opening a jagged gap in the gloom that just as quickly slams shut again. I pause briefly to put up my hood and zip my parka. Pamola is somewhere hereabouts, beating his wings, kicking up a modest tempest. Dressed in full winter gear—hat, mitts, pile, shells—I reach the top of the spur and enter the strange, gently rising, boulder-studded, moorlike expanse of the tablelands sweeping toward the summit.

In Baxter State Park, a mauve-colored boulder rises out of Daicey Pond after a passing thunderstorm.

Thoreau got about this far on his 1846 attempt. As he climbed, the clouds closed around him, blotting out the sky, and cold winds swept the stark moonscape before him. In this surreal wasteland he encountered a different nature than the gentle one he knew from wandering the forests and fields of Concord.

On Katahdin, for the first time, Thoreau came face to face with true wilderness, a place with a wild spirit not yet tamed by humanity. Here, Thoreau realized, nature was utterly indifferent to his fate.

Thoreau was both terrified and yet strangely thrilled by this contact with a power greater than any he had ever felt before. His experience on Katahdin caused him to examine his own existence. Later, he wrote movingly of his time on the mountain: "Talk of mysteries! Think of our life in nature, daily to be shown matter, to come in contact with it—rocks, trees, wind on our cheeks! The *solid* earth! The *actual* world. The *common* sense. *Contact! Contact! Who* are we? *Where* are we?"

The intervening century and a half has brought little change. Katahdin still stands indomitable above the forest wilderness of Maine. At any time of year Pamola may humble even the best trained and equipped climbing parties. In Baxter State Park in winter, which lasts five months, temperatures can plunge into the minus forties, and winter storms often drop heavy loads of snow. At this time of year the

Fiery sugar maple leaves and white paper birch trunks create pleasing color contrasts in autumn in the White Mountains of New Hampshire.

North Woods of Maine is a particularly harsh reminder of human frailty. This wildest corner of the lower forty-eight states rarely fails to remind the visitor that nature is in control.

At the summit, a handful of hikers are milling around the cairn marking the end of the Appalachian Trail. A young couple, a father and young son, a middle-aged dentist from Georgia—they snap a few pictures then duck for cover behind boulders. Seeking shelter, I crouch in the lee of the summit ridge, and devour a hurried lunch while taking in the expansive view of the Great Basin, an enormous horseshoe-shaped cirque chiseled out of the mountains by glaciers during the last ice age fifteen thousand years ago. On all sides of this gigantic amphitheater, precipitous walls plunge from the sharply serrated ridgelines down to the basin floor. The scene is impossibly alpine, rockier than the Rockies.

Lunch finished, I stand and absorb the 360-degree view of the Maine Woods from the peak, recalling again Thoreau's words from this very mountain 150 years ago: "From this elevation," he wrote, "just on the skirts of the clouds, we could overlook the country . . . for a hundred miles. There it was, the State of Maine. . . . Immeasurable forest. . . . Countless lakes . . . like . . . a mirror broken into a thousand fragments, and wildly scattered . . . reflecting the full blaze of the sun."

For a long moment I gaze upon the seemingly endless forest of Maine. I look out at Caribou Lake; Chesuncook Lake; and far beyond them to where the Allagash and St. John rivers flow north to the Canadian border. And then, as I cautiously begin the descent of the precipitous Knife Edge trail, looking down a thousand feet on either side, I once again give silent thanks to the vision, courage, and tenacity of Percival P. Baxter.

Facing page
The snow-dusted branches of hardwood trees reach into the frigid skies of a late-December morning in the White Mountains.

Left
The oranges, reds, and yellows of a New England autumn are illuminated at sunset on a Vermont hillside.

Above
Lush beech leaves stretch across the tumbling waters of the Ompomponoosuc River in Vermont.

Facing page
The mixed hardwood forest reaches across the Upper Connecticut River Valley in Vermont to the foothills of New Hampshire's White Mountains in the distance.

Above
Peeling birch bark unfurls in the bitter cold of a Green Mountain winter.

Left
The trunks of a mixed hardwood forest cast long shadows over the snow in the early afternoon of a midwinter Vermont day.

Facing page
A full palette of autumn colors carpets the forest floor along the Appalachian Trail in the Upper Connecticut River Valley of Vermont.

Left
Sunlight illuminates the bark of a hemlock tree on a Vermont afternoon in winter.

Below
Tiger lilies line the banks of Vermont's White River in summer.

Above
Water tumbles through the lush forest in Granville Gulf in the heart of the Green Mountains.

Right
The dry, dead skeletons of spruce trees rise from the beaver pond that drowned them deep in the forest of Vermont's Northeast Kingdom.

Autumn leaves grace a little rivulet near the Appalachian Trail in Vermont.

Left
Fog enshrouds the forested flanks of Mount Paugus in New Hampshire's White Mountains.

Above
The White Mountains live up to their name as fresh, wind-sculpted snow blankets a frozen wetland in New Hampshire.

Above
A wisp of paper birch bark and colorful autumn leaves litter the forest floor in the White Mountains.

Left
A red maple leaf rests upon dewy meadow grass in New Hampshire.

Above
A white birch tree rises from the lush green understory in Jefferson Notch, White Mountains.

Right
The rich mixed forest of deciduous and coniferous trees extends across the undulating peaks of the White Mountain National Forest.

Draped, chili-colored sumac leaves are resplendent on an October morning in southern New Hampshire.

Summer sunlight pours through the canopy of a mature mixed forest in Bash Bish Falls State Park in the Berkshires of Massachusetts.

The Housatonic River has carved an impressive gorge through the hard bedrock at Bulls Bridge in the Litchfield Hills of Connecticut.

The feathery branches of white pines reach across a mountain pond at sunset in Mohawk State Forest of northwestern Connecticut.

Golden sunlight illuminates the trunk of a conifer in the forest along the banks of Maine's Allagash River.

Chapter 3

THE RIVERS AND LAKES

ALLAGASH WILDERNESS WATERWAY

Above
Cascading rapids bubble wildly on Maine's Penobscot River.

Left
The pristine waters of a freshwater pond in Rhode Island's Burlingame
State Park reflect the golden glow of sunset.

IN NORTHERN MAINE, several hours by truck over rough logging roads from the nearest settlement, a vast network of interconnected lakes, rivers, and streams flows through the heart of one of America's last great uninterrupted forests. In the headwaters of this system, small brooks wind through swampy beaver flowages, tangled alder hells, and between rocky ridges crowned with northern hardwoods. Gathering strength, these tributaries pour into the chain of ponds and lakes from which flows the great river itself.

This is the Allagash Wilderness Waterway, and as my friend Dan and I are discovering, it's a classic canoe-country adventure. The big lakes are lovely, with mile after mile of undeveloped wooded shoreline. In camp at night we hear the ghostly, haunting cry of a loon as we sit mesmerized by the flickering flames of the campfire. On several nights, the northern lights have blazed across the sky. During the day we frequently see moose and deer feeding in the shallows of the lakes and feeder streams, and for much of the distance as we paddle we can see Katahdin rising like a carved stone monument high above the treetops.

Used as a travel route by generations of Native Americans, loggers, outfitters, and guides, the Allagash is truly imbued with the spirit of the North Country, and it offers the wilderness traveler the chance to experience life in the wilds at the more measured pace of an earlier era.

Henry David Thoreau paddled the big headwater lakes of the Allagash in the mid-1800s, and he was so moved by the experience that he issued a call to have the region set aside as a wilderness preserve long before the world's first national park, Yellowstone, was created. In *The Maine Woods*, Thoreau wrote: "Why should not we . . . have our national preserves . . . in which the bear and the panther, and

Right
Seboomook Lake forms a large swath of blue amidst the forest of green deep in northern Maine.

Facing page
The Housatonic River traverses a boulder-studded rapid in Connecticut's Litchfield Hills on its 150-mile journey from western Massachusetts to Long Island Sound.

some even of the hunter race, may still exist, and not be 'civilized off the face of the earth.'"

A little more than a century later, in 1966, the Allagash Wilderness Waterway was set aside by the people of Maine when they voted to support a bond protecting its wilderness character. In 1970, the Allagash's special qualities were recognized by the federal government, and the waterway was designated a National Wild and Scenic River. Today, the Allagash is a superb example of the rich network of rivers and lakes that connects each part of New England to every other.

Rain-swollen Texas Brook flows through the Green Mountains near Middlebury Gap on a damp autumn day.

New England is blessed with an unusual wealth of lakes and ponds, rivers and streams. From Lake Champlain to Grand Falls Flowage, and from Otter Creek to the St. Croix River, New England is crisscrossed by waterways flowing from the mountains to the sea. Many of these rivers—such as the St. John, the Penobscot, the Kennebec, the Saco, the Merrimack, the Housatonic, and the Connecticut—drain huge watersheds that served as critical transportation routes and corridors for exploration, settlement, and commerce.

Each of these rivers ultimately flows into the ocean, emptying into coastal estuaries such as Long Island Sound off the Connecticut coast; Narragansett Bay off Rhode Island; Buzzards Bay off Massachusetts; Casco Bay off Portland, Maine; and Great Bay near Portsmouth, New Hampshire. These and numerous other smaller estuaries are critical nurseries for marine life; they provide tremendous recreational opportunities enjoyed by millions of New Englanders; and they support a storied fishing fleet that has employed generations of Yankees for nearly four hundred years.

For the Native Americans, these innumerable rivers and lakes were transportation routes that took them to their hunting and fishing grounds, to trade with or make war upon distant villages, or to travel upstream to the woods and downstream to the sea according to the cycle of the seasons. Using the vast labyrinth of waterways, it was—and still is—possible to travel from one end of New England to the other. As Thoreau noted when he traveled the Maine Woods: "The country is an archipelago of lakes—the lake-country of New England. Their levels vary but a few feet, and the boatmen, by short portages, or by none at all, pass easily from one to another."

And as Thoreau and countless others have discovered, for poking around in the watery New England wilds you really can't beat canoe travel. What the horse is to the Westerner, the canoe is to the New Englander: the traditional mode of transportation in the wilderness. Light, simple, elegant, and strong enough to carry heavy loads, the canoe was and still is the vehicle of choice for exploring a region laced by countless lakes, rivers, and streams.

The canoe gets you farther into the New England wild faster and lets you stay out there longer than any other form of nonmotorized transportation. The vessel was invented here in these woodlands by Abenaki craftsmen, who built the nimble little boats out of birch bark. Small wonder European explorers adopted the canoe when they set out to explore the continent; their sluggish, heavy rowboats were useless on inland waters and impracticable for carrying on portages, and the swift canoes paddled circles around them. Not only that, but the natives faced forward and could see where they were going. The Old World took a bow to superior New World technology.

A canoe trip in the New England wilds is not only the best way to explore the region's natural landscapes; it's a chance for viewing wildlife along the shorelines of the rivers and lakes. Seeing moose is an anticipated highlight of most trips in the north, but the forest is home to other creatures as well. Deer are plentiful, as are bear, bobcat, beaver, raccoon, and porcupine. In the north, sharp-eyed paddlers may see a rare Canada lynx or a pine marten. Sometime in your travels you are likely to be serenaded by coyotes, and of course the cry of the loon is the voice of this northern wilderness.

As Thoreau noted in *The Maine Woods*: "In the middle of the night, as indeed each time that we lay on the shore of a lake, we heard the voice of the loon, loud and distinct, from far over the lake. It is a very wild sound, quite in keeping with the place and the circumstances of the traveler, and very unlike the voice of a bird. I could lie awake for several hours listening to it, it is so thrilling."

Besides loons, canoeists also have an excellent chance of seeing terns, kingfishers, great blue herons, woodcock, ruffed grouse, ospreys, bald eagles, and a rich assortment of ducks and songbirds. Canoe parties that move quietly, especially at dawn and dusk, stand the best chance of encountering wildlife in the lakes, rivers, and streams.

The fishing, too, is often superb, and unlike in some other parts of the country, many of the fish populations are wild, not stocked. Brook trout, known locally as "squaretails," are found in streams and ponds throughout the region, while lake trout, often called "togue," are found in the cold, clean, deep waters of the larger lakes.

Dan and I began our journey by paddling down the upper part of Allagash Stream to the inlet at Allagash Lake. Ringed by mountains and glaciated rock ledges and sprinkled with emerald islands, the lake is one of the most remote and beautiful lakes in the waterway. And now, taking our time to soak in the view, we paddle the three and a half miles across the sparkling blue surface from the inlet to the outlet of Allagash Stream, catching a couple of togue along the way where the lake reaches a depth of nearly ninety feet.

Allagash Stream is pure delight, and for the next five miles we rock and roll down this tight, boulder-filled whitewater run, practicing our tandem maneuvers even though the boat is a little sluggish, loaded down with a week's worth of food

High in the White Mountains, autumn reflections turn the waters of the Swift River the color of molten lava.

and camping gear. At Little Allagash Falls, where the stream drops twenty feet over a rocky outcrop, we make the short carry before riding the waves again down to Chamberlain Lake, the largest in the waterway.

Chamberlain is big, roughly twenty miles long, and with its northwest–southeast orientation it puts paddlers directly in the path of the prevailing winds sweeping down from the northwest. No wonder the Abenaki called it *Apmoojenegomook*, or "Lake that is Crossed" (in a hurry). Dan and I paddle hard, fighting the wind to get over to the eastern shore, where there is a half-mile portage to Eagle Lake, the second largest in the waterway. Here, on shore, out of the wind, and out of the canoe, we walk the portage, and near the Eagle Lake end of the trail, we come upon one of the oddest scenes imaginable: Here, in the middle of the Great North Woods, some seventy-five miles from the nearest railroad, are two full-size, ninety-ton steam locomotives. They—along with the track, bolts, clamps, cables, and tons of other hardware—were brought to this incongruous spot over the ice in the winter and assembled here to pull freight cars filled with pulpwood the twelve and a half miles from Umbazooksus Lake to Chamberlain Lake. At Chamberlain, the logs were floated into the Penobscot River system and eventually to the mills in Bangor. Despite the monumental effort to get them here, the trains had a relatively short career: they began running in 1927 and were abandoned by 1937.

Two days after crossing Chamberlain Lake, we make the short portage around Churchill Dam by the Ranger cabin and enter the Allagash River itself at Chase Rapids—four miles of whitewater between Churchill Lake and Umsaskis Lake. It's a raw, cold, cheerless day with leaden skies and spritzers of rain, but the rapids, which are usually rated a mild Class III in the guidebooks, lift our spirits with their rambunctiousness.

Before starting down Chase Rapids, I read a description of the river ahead, and I learn that it was here, in December 1901, that hunters made one of the last authenticated sightings of woodland caribou in Maine. (There have since been two attempts to re-establish the Maine caribou herd, in 1963 and 1988. Unfortunately, both failed, apparently due to black-bear predation.)

When we enter the rapids, the water grabs the hull and pulls it downstream with vigor. Dan and I back-paddle hard, slowing the canoe and keeping the bow from spearing into the heavy waves. Without shipping a drop, we deftly guide the loaded craft through the chutes and drops, emerging onto Umsaskis around midday.

From the headwater lakes, the Allagash flows almost due north for another seventy miles, alternating between fast water, meandering channels, and an occasional deadwater such as Round Pond or Finley Bogan. And as the days go by, I

Sabbaday Falls comes tumbling out of the high White Mountains near Kancamagus Pass in central New Hampshire.

not only have the feeling of traveling deeper into the wilds with every paddle stroke, but also of going back in time to an age when all travel was like this—at a human pace, and through an untarnished natural landscape. Thoreau felt the same way when he was in the Maine Woods, writing: "It reminded me of Prometheus Bound. Here was traveling of the old heroic kind over the unaltered face of nature."

The Allagash saves the best for last. As Dan and I wind through the low islands of Finley Bogan, we can hear a low roar drifting up toward us on the wind. The sound is coming from downstream, and we have no doubt what is causing it. The current picks up and speeds toward the sound. As the volume increases, we angle the canoe toward the right bank and get out for the portage around Allagash Falls.

Allagash Falls is a magnificent thirty-foot cascade where the entire river funnels through a narrow slot in a high rock ridge and empties into the St. John River for the next leg of the journey to the sea. The portage is short, and at the bottom we stand on river-scoured, polished rock pocked with round potholes carved over millennia by the rushing water. While Dan hooks up with several salmon in the tailrace below the torrent, I just sit on the rock and look back up at the falls, one of the most spectacular I have ever seen, replaying in my mind's eye the many sights and splendors I have witnessed along this fabulous vestige of New England's—and all America's—wild waterways.

The tree-lined waters of Norton Pond rise just south of the Canadian border in Vermont's Northeast Kingdom.

Above
A cow moose wades in the shallows of the appropriately named Moose River.

Left
Morning mist rises above the West Branch of the Penobscot River.

Rocks and aquatic greenery near the shores of Upper Richardson Lake in Maine.

The West Branch of the Penobscot River gathers force as it heads through the Cribworks, a powerful rapid in the Maine Woods.

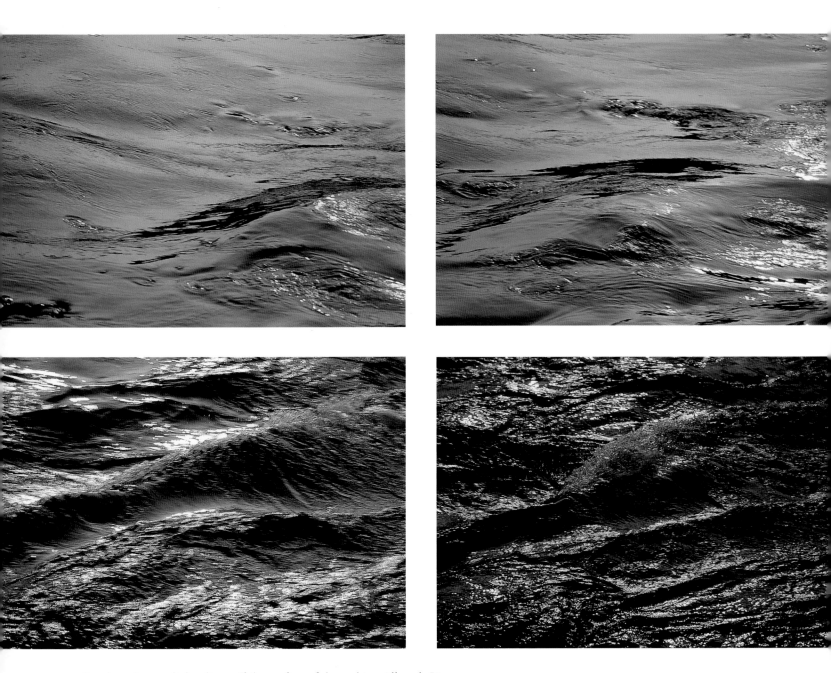

Late-evening sunlight glints off the surface of the rushing Allagash River.

Screw Auger Falls drops down to the west branch of the Pleasant River in Gulf Hagas Preserve, Maine.

Colorful foliage is perfectly reflected on the surface of Little Lake on a stunning autumn day in the White Mountains.

Fiery sugar maple leaves stretch out above the rapids on New Hampshire's Swift River.

Zealand Falls flows heavily on a blustery October afternoon in the White Mountains.

A hidden waterfall pours over boulders in Jefferson Brook, high on Jefferson Notch in New Hampshire.

A rustic footbridge crosses the rocky east branch of New Hampshire's Pemigewasset River in the rich light of an autumn afternoon.

The White River in central Vermont is calm on a cloudy summer afternoon.

One of the headwater streams of the White River flows through the veil-like cascade of Moss Glen Falls in Granville Gulf Reservation, Green Mountain National Forest.

Above
Falls Brook pours over a cataract into a cool mountain pool in Kent Falls State Park, Connecticut.

Right
A red sugar maple leaf is submerged in the Mad River in Green Mountain National Forest.

Cattails blow in the warm summer breeze on the shore of Washining Lake in the Berkshire Hills of northwestern Connecticut.

Left, top
Twin veils of water pour down from a pool above in Bash Bish Falls State Park, Massachusetts.

Left, bottom
Spear-like tips of watery vegetation catch the last light in a backwater slough on the Upper Connecticut River in New Hampshire.

Far left
This wild mountain pond is peaceful on a fair summer afternoon in the Litchfield Hills of Connecticut.

A great blue heron stalks a salt pond at dusk near Matunuk Beach on the Rhode Island shore.

Ghostly rocks emerge out of the gentle swells of a freshwater pond in Burlingame State Park, Rhode Island.

Chapter 4

THE MOUNTAINS

APPALACHIAN TRAIL

Above
The crystal waters of a mountain spring splash down the sheer rocky face of Vermont's Mount Pisgah.

Left
The bare alpine summits of the Presidential Range rise above the clouds on an early winter morning.

WE AWOKE EXPECTING a fair day, but unzipped the tent to find we were socked in by clouds. The sky was a uniform gray, visibility limited to our immediate environs. The gnarled trees alternately appeared and disappeared, wraithlike, in the ghostly fog. Wasting no time, we ate a hurried breakfast and took to the trail.

The path led upward, first through solid hardwoods and then through the transition zone into the conifers. It was a cool, blustery midsummer day, and there was a wet, secretive hush in the woods, so we proceeded watchfully, cautiously, trying not to break the spell. Without grand vistas and scenic overlooks, we noticed the little things, such as the moisture trapped and shimmering on spider webs in the branches of the trees, and the silver beads of water on the leaves of blue-bead lily.

Toward midafternoon, we were closing in on the tree line, but the infamous winds of New Hampshire's White Mountains were whipping the Presidential Range with ragged clouds. My friend Steve and I had already ascended for miles, and now we faced the day's toughest decision: whether to proceed above tree line to the summit of Mount Washington, or find a suitable spot for a bivouac somewhere below tree line and away from the elements.

New England's mountains once rivaled the Himalaya, but two hundred million years have elapsed since then, and the ravages of time have worn them to their present stature, leaving 6,288-foot Mount Washington as the highest peak. Yet, don't be deceived. Though they are no longer as high as they once were, New England's mountains are still impressively tall from base to summit, starting as they do so close to sea level. It might well surprise Westerners to learn that, for example, the vertical gain of New Hampshire's Mount Adams (5,798 feet above sea level) is greater than that for Colorado's Mount Elbert (14,433 feet above sea level), the highest peak in the Rockies.

The summit of Mount Washington was a several-mile, several-thousand-foot climb, which would put us at the top right around sundown—not a good option. And yet I was anxious for tree line. All day I had hiked through the green tunnel, burrowing along like a mole under a canopy of spruce, fir, birch, and fog. But to risk going above the forest boundary into the exposed region of rock and lichen in the alpine zone would be foolish. Besides, since visibility on top was limited to only a few yards, we would completely miss the views from the high peaks.

Decision made, the next task was to find a place to put up the tent. We needed a flat spot a couple of hundred feet off the trail, as required by the regulations. We also needed to find water for drinking and cooking, not an easy chore high in the White Mountains.

Apparently other hikers had faced the same decision, and by following a faint trail into the forest we discovered a serviceable spot for the tent. We located water

Tuckerman Ravine on Mount Washington receives copious amounts of snow throughout the winter. In especially snowy years, the many gullies and chutes remain snow-stuffed well into June.

by following a dry gully about a hundred yards down the slope. There we came to a wet, mossy glade where water pooled before continuing its slow seep down the mountain.

Steve and I reached our position below the summit of Mount Washington by following the Crawford Path, in White Mountain National Forest. Originally a bridle trail built by Abel and Ethan Crawford in 1819, Crawford Path is the oldest continuously maintained trail in the United States. The path begins in rugged Crawford Notch then climbs some eight and a half miles through one of the wildest and most scenic landscapes in the region to the top of Mount Washington. It is a rigorous trail. The final five miles are entirely above the tree line and cross the largest alpine zone in eastern North America south of Labrador. Up there, climbers are fully exposed and vulnerable to the fury of the frequent storm systems that strike the range.

When the Crawfords built their path in the early nineteenth century, there were no purely hiking trails leading to the heights, only paths built for horses. Hiking was not something many people did for pleasure until decades later, and fashionable outdoorsmen and -women much preferred riding their mounts to the

Stunted, rime-coated conifers rise above the wind-scoured snowpack on the summit ridge of Mount Moosilauke on a frigid, subzero winter day in the White Mountains.

In spring, Glen Ellis Falls pours like a silvery cascade at Pinkham Notch, some 1,900 feet above sea level in the White Mountains.

summits, even though the precipitous White Mountains were hardly more equine-friendly territory then than they are now.

From Crawford Notch, the trail passes Gibbs Falls and the Gibbs Brook Scenic Area, which is home to the largest virgin stand of spruce and birch in New England. Farther on, the Crawford Path traverses several ledges offering magnificent views of the Presidential Range. Still higher, the trail passes the summit of Mount Monroe before reaching the Lakes of the Clouds, a spectacular glacial tarn set among jumbled boulders. From there, the Crawford Path begins the final ascent of the summit cone of Mount Washington.

When I began the long climb, I was both filled with admiration for the Crawfords and puzzled about why they would undertake the monumental task of building the route. Climbing the trail is tough; constructing it must have been backbreaking. Hauling myself up the mountain, I am consoled by the thought that the Crawfords had horses, and I felt better for a while.

This path is a portion of the Appalachian Trail, known to those who love it as simply the "AT." The AT winds along the wild crest of the Appalachian Mountains for 2,135 miles, making it likely the longest marked footpath in the world. Managed by the National Park Service, the trail extends from Springer Mountain in northern Georgia to Mount Katahdin, the giant, granite monolith rising above the vast boreal forests of northern Maine.

Along the way from Georgia to Maine, the trail follows the skyline, touching the tops of most states it enters. In New England, the AT traverses several distinct ranges that make up the Appalachian chain in this region, including the Green Mountains, the White Mountains, the Taconic Range, the Berkshire Hills, and several other lesser-known ranges. Each range has its own unique geologic history and personality that makes it memorable to the foot traveler.

The Green Mountains and Vermont are synonymous, for the word "Vermont" is a French contraction for "green mountain." The Green Mountains are a long range of rounded, wooded peaks and ridges stretching the length of the state, from Massachusetts in the south to Quebec in the north. Although primarily a continuous

By mid-September the foliage surrounding the bald-faced peaks of the White Mountains begins to adopt its autumn hues.

A Vermont hillside in the Upper Connecticut River Valley is in peak foliage on a glorious and crisp autumn afternoon.

range of forested ridgelines, there are many places in the Green Mountains where the rocky summits rise above the trees as truly impressive peaks.

The Taconic Mountains run along the western border of Massachusetts and southwestern Vermont, bordering the Berkshires and Green Mountains to the east. The highest peak in the Taconics is Mount Equinox, which rises to an elevation of 3,816 feet at the northern end of the range in Manchester, Vermont.

The Berkshires of western Massachusetts and northwestern Connecticut is a region of wooded hills, lakes, rivers, and streams defined by the Hoosic River valley to the north, the Housatonic River valley to the south, and the Taconic Range to the west. The Berkshires are essentially the southern extension of the Green Mountains, but the name "Berkshires" is generally used when describing the highlands of western Massachusetts and northwestern Connecticut. The highest peak in the range is Mount Greylock, which rises to an elevation of 3,491 feet near Williamstown.

The Appalachian Trail visits each of these ranges, running along the spines of the Taconics, the Berkshires, and the Green Mountains before leaving Vermont at Norwich, crossing the Connecticut River into Hanover, and then quickly heading up into the White Mountains of New Hampshire.

Though the AT seeks the high, wild country above the more settled valleys of New England, the trail does maintain occasional contact with the towns and peopled landscapes below. This relationship is deliberate, and it was an essential part of the original thinking that ultimately produced the Appalachian Trail.

Many people hold incorrect ideas concerning the origins of this famous pathway, owing perhaps to the universal nature of foot travel and the supposition that the trail has always been there in one shape or another. Some believe the AT was an ancient track used by hunting, trading, and warring parties before and during the Colonial Era. Others suppose it must have been a sequence of rough roads used by armies and pioneers during the early years of our nation's history. Not so.

Although the trail does occasionally employ sections of historic byways such as the Crawford Path, for the most part the AT is not a series of old tracks stitched together into a continuous whole. Virtually the entire trail was laid out and cut by the hands of volunteers during the years leading up to World War II.

The idea for an Appalachian Trail was first proposed in 1921 by Benton MacKaye of Massachusetts. An ardent hiker and outdoorsman, MacKaye believed wilderness outings conferred beneficial effects on the physical and mental health of an increasingly urban and sedentary population.

By late autumn, the first storms have already dropped several inches of new snow in the White Mountains.

During his long rambles in the New England mountains, MacKaye dreamed of a path running the entire length of the eastern seaboard. He envisioned a wild trail, yet one well within reach of major urban centers and the throngs of workers who lived there and who were increasingly alienated from nature. He felt the trail would grace all who spent time on it with the healing tonic of wilderness, and he wanted it to be accessible to everyone. MacKaye articulated his vision in an article entitled "An Appalachian Trail, A Project in Regional Planning," published in the October 1921 issue of the *Journal of the American Institute of Architects*. The response to his idea was swift and supportive.

Hiking clubs along the proposed route picked up MacKaye's idea, and in less than a year the first miles of the AT were constructed by volunteers in the Bear Mountain section in New York. Soon, volunteers from Maine to Georgia were hard at work building the trail. Their energy and enthusiasm for turning his vision into reality surprised even MacKaye.

Under the leadership first of MacKaye, then later Arthur Perkins, a Connecticut judge, and especially Myron Avery, a stubborn lawyer from Lubec, Maine—who insisted that the trail end at Katahdin and not New Hampshire's Mount Washington—the Appalachian Trail was pushed through to completion by 1937. Avery, the first to walk the entire length of the trail, said in a speech: "To say that the Trail is completed would be a complete misnomer. Those of us, who have physically worked on the trail, know that the trail, as such, will never be completed." Avery expressed what thousands have since learned: The trail is not merely a line drawn upon a map; hiking it is an experience with reverberations that last a lifetime.

Fortunately, MacKaye, who lived until 1975 and died just short of his ninety-seventh birthday, was able to watch his dream become reality. After many decades of association with the trail, he wrote: "The ultimate purpose? There are three things: 1) to walk; 2) to see; 3) to *see* what you see. . . . Some people like to record how speedily they can traverse the length of the trail, but I would give a prize for the ones who took the longest time."

As Steve and I took our time settling in for the night in our camp below tree line, we watched the sun drop behind tattered clouds toward the jagged peaks to the west. Shafts of light poured through rifts in the clouds, each beam distinct, spotlighting the black borders of the mountains. Eventually, the red ball of the sun broke free and disappeared beyond the ranges, but the fiery glow held us captive for quite a while before the last light faded and the stars emerged overhead.

That night, sheltered in the thick forest of stunted evergreens, we heard the wind roaring through the treetops just yards overhead. One moment we could

As snow blankets the landscape, the Deerfield River flows through Zoar Gap in the Berkshire Hills.

see the Big Dipper pointing to the North Star, but the next instant the sky was completely obscured by a rushing train of gray, wispy vapor.

Dawn broke to bright, sunny skies. Though the wind was still cool and brisk, we were graced with a rare clear day in the Presidential Range—mountains that are notorious for having the world's worst weather and have claimed the lives of well over a hundred travelers since Frederick Strickland was caught by a sudden winter storm in October 1851.

As we ascended, the little trees give way to Krummholz, the stunted evergreen growth that survives in this environment only because it spreads outward, not upward, remaining insulated beneath the snowpack in winter. Soon, even the Krummholz was gone, replaced by rock, lichen, and sedge. The trail stumbled over frost-blasted rock shards and was marked by sentinel-like cairns of stone marching across the open area known as the Bigelow Lawn.

The final push to the summit was a steep boulder-hop where the painted trail blazes marked only one of a multitude of possible routes up. All semblance of a trail disappeared in the chaos of the massive rockfall. I chose a more zigzag path than the one prescribed, taking a less direct but ultimately easier path to the top.

And then we were there, high atop the roof of New England at 6,288 feet. The view to the north and east was of endless rows of mountains interrupted by forested valleys, and somewhere out there Benton MacKaye's trail kept going and going beyond the horizon. When we looked to the south and west, however, roiling clouds warned us of another approaching storm. Our grace period was over, and we took one last look around, and then scurried down the trail to tree line once again, heading north toward Katahdin.

Mountains along the Maine-Quebec border rise above Attean Pond at sunset in the Maine Woods.

Above

New Hampshire's Presidential Range is known for having the world's worst weather. Winds of over 230 miles per hour have been clocked on the summit of Mount Washington.

Left

A long, snowy couloir runs down from the ridgeline of Mount Washington on a clear April morning.

The Swift River flows down from the heights of Kancamagus Pass in the White Mountains on an autumn day.

Sunrise strikes the snowy summit of Mount Washington on an early December morning.

Above
A winter blizzard coats Mount Moosilauke with another layer of snow in the White Mountains.

Right
The snowy, craggy summits of Lafayette Ridge rise above Franconia Notch in the heart of the White Mountains.

The wilderness surrounding Mount Chocorua's rocky summit transforms with the seasons, high above the shores of Chocorua Lake in the White Mountain National Forest.

Left
The sheer cliffs of Mount Pisgah rise directly above the waters of Lake Willoughby in Vermont's Northeast Kingdom.

Above
Gnarled, cracked, lichen-covered granite characterizes the summit of Camels Hump in the Green Mountains.

Facing page
A rich palette of color infuses the sky above Mount Katahdin at sunset on a February evening.

Above, top
Spring runoff swells a powerful waterfall crashing out of the southern Green Mountains.

Above, bottom
Looking north along the spine of the Green Mountains, from Mount Ellen to Camels Hump to Mount Mansfield.

The White River rises in the heart of the Green Mountains and cuts a rugged cleft in the hills on its way to a junction with the Connecticut River.

A long crack in the ice of Chimney Pond stretches toward Mount Katahdin's Knife Edge in Maine's Baxter State Park.

Chapter 5

THE GREAT BEACH

CAPE COD NATIONAL SEASHORE

Above
A wave advances onto the sandy shore.

Left
A great sweep of empty beach. The Outer Cape is some seventy miles out to sea from the mainland of Massachusetts.

Like a great, sharp hook, Massachusetts's Cape Cod thrusts east and then north for some seventy miles, farther into the Atlantic than any other portion of the continental United States. Standing atop the windswept dunes of Wellfleet in 1855, gazing out to the storm-tossed Atlantic, Henry David Thoreau reflected that "a man may stand here and put all America behind him." For a few precious days, as summer green alchemized into autumn gold, I set out to see if a man still could.

Legs pumping, heart pounding, chest heaving with each explosive breath, I struggled to maintain balance and forward momentum up the steep, narrow trail. We had been riding for hours on lonely, unmarked single-track and deserted overgrown fire roads, winding around the cool freshwater ponds and through the tinder-dry oak and pitch-pine forest of the Outer Cape. As the warm sun approached its midday zenith, one last hill stood between us and our goal.

I pedaled rapidly to a rhythmic cadence pounding like a kettle drum in my head, a simple mantra that matched each quick stroke of the crank and went "Push. Push. Push." Meanwhile, somewhere in the background, a familiar chorus urged me on, chanting "Don't stop. Don't walk." With arm and leg muscles burning from the strain, I began to reel in the last painful yards to the top of the hill, following my wife, Mary, and our dog, Tasha, who had already topped out.

The grade steepened, and the rear tire started to lose traction, slipping badly. I downshifted to my lowest, last-chance gear a second too late, straining the derailleur with a merciless, high-powered torque "*Crunch*" yet maintaining just enough headway to churn over the rise and coast out of the forest shade into the blinding white sunshine.

Ahead, a sandy path led through the swaying, emerald beach grasses toward lofty dunes. Moments later, atop the escarpment, we sucked greedily on our water bottles and looked out at the limitless Atlantic, watched the waves roll in with a thunderous roar more than a hundred feet below. The breakers crashed down upon the Great Beach, an unbroken strand lying between the dunes and the sea and stretching to the horizon for miles in both directions. And in all that vast, sandy, salty distance, there was no one else in sight.

The notion of Cape Cod as wild may strike some as oxymoronic, and with good reason. After all, the Cape lies within a day's drive of one-quarter of the nation's population, and ever since European explorers first sailed here in the early seventeenth century, Cape Cod has hardly qualified as undiscovered country. Any veteran of weekend-traffic combat on Route 6, or anyone else who has spent an afternoon trying to extricate himself from the ticky-tacky tangle of cheap development that blights so much of the roadside environment here might well believe the Cape is among the very last places Americans would go to find solitude and replenish their souls.

But if you get off the highway on the Outer Cape, if you get out of the car, you will discover a very different Cape Cod than the one seen through the tinted-

From high upon the dunes of Cape Cod, Henry David Thoreau looked out upon the Atlantic and said, "A man may stand here and put all America behind him."

glass windshield. The stretch of land from the Cape's southeastern tip at Chatham to the northern apex at Provincetown has a pace and mood far removed from the roar of traffic and the neon come-ons of Falmouth and Hyannis. Here on the Outer Cape is a realm of striking solitude and surprising diversity. Here is a captivating wild of pounding surf, towering dunes, and fertile marshes, of solitary stands of Atlantic white cedar, of upland fields and pastures. Here too are hundreds of glacially formed kettle ponds and lakes fringed by oak and pine forests.

And then, of course, here is the Great Beach. For more than thirty miles, it stretches unbroken and undeveloped along the ocean wilderness.

This is brand-new territory, geologically speaking, for it was only some fifteen thousand years ago that bulldozing glaciers piled up this great ridge of sand, silt, and rubble—a giant dumping ground geologists call a terminal moraine. As the glaciers melted, the sea rose, nearly drowning the newly created mound of debris. Once free of its heavy ice burden, however, the moraine rebounded, gradually rising hundreds of feet above the waves. Over the course of the last ten thousand years, wind and tide have completed shaping the moraine into the Cape Cod we know today.

And yet nothing stays the same, and every visitor to the Cape will witness, and participate in, the ongoing process of transformation. Each footfall on the sand, every wave and gust of wind, continues the task of reshaping Cape Cod. According to the geologists, at some point far in the future the sea will vanquish the dunes and all that will remain of the Cape will be a few scattered islands far out to sea.

Even though this is new territory from a geologic standpoint, it is yet an old place, this Cape Cod, having been settled by Europeans for nearly four hundred years and inhabited long prior to that by Native Americans. For some ten thousand years the Wampanoag inhabited the peninsula, making a living from the sea while also cultivating corn, beans, and other crops in the sandy soil. Many of the familiar Cape Cod place-names— Nauset, Pamet, Monomoy—were given by these Native Americans.

In 1602, a mariner named Bartholomew Gosnold cruised past the great sandy peninsula and noted that the waters were rich in codfish. He jotted the name "Cape Cod" to his chart before sailing by. The name stuck. Later, while searching for a new home, the Pilgrims coasted the Cape aboard the *Mayflower*. They landed in Provincetown Harbor in November 1620. There, they drew up the Mayflower Compact, the early constitution that eventually gave birth to the Commonwealth of Massachusetts. From Provincetown, the Pilgrims moved on to found Plymouth, across Cape Cod Bay.

Some of the Pilgrims, impressed by what they had seen of the Cape, left Plymouth and moved back out to the great, sandy reaches. There they established

Beach vegetation thrives in sheltered areas at the foot of the dunes at Cape Cod National Seashore.

the steadfast communities of Yankee whalers, fishermen, and farmers whose descendants populate the Cape to this day. English place names—Pilgrim Heights, Pilgrim Spring Trail, First Encounter Beach—testify to the presence of these early settlers.

The original Yankees were later joined by fishermen from the coast and islands of Portugal, and together they scratched a living from the sandy soil; plied the waters for a seemingly endless supply of lobsters, cod, scallops, clams, bluefish, whales, and other marine life; manned lifeguard stations and lighthouses; and occasionally salvaged small fortunes from the nearly three thousand ships that foundered on the Cape's treacherous shoals. The Outer Cape was once considered the most dangerous passage in all of North America, until the opening of the Cape Cod Canal in 1914, connecting Buzzards Bay in the south to Cape Cod Bay in the north, which allowed ships to traverse tranquil interior waters rather than risk the dangerous route around the Cape.

In the first few decades of the twentieth century, New Englanders began the tradition of going "down to the Cape" for the summer. There they swam in the surf, walked the empty beaches, sailed the calm bay waters, and held clambakes on the sandy shore. The Cape became what it remains today: a popular vacationing place, somewhere to go to refresh body and soul.

The Cape also attracted a creative and offbeat element that might have felt constrained in a more genteel setting. Artists such as Jackson Pollack and Edward Hopper, writers such as Jack Kerouac and Eugene O'Neill, and actors such as Humphrey Bogart and Orson Welles were drawn to the Cape by its restorative qualities and the liberal, accepting attitudes of the natives.

By the 1950s, however, the Cape was suffering from its own popularity. Much of the Upper Cape, the area around Woods Hole and Falmouth, had become exactly

A wave rolls up on the beach in Truro, near the northern end of the Cape.

The Provincelands is a vast stretch of sand extending for miles between the Great Beach and the town of Provincetown.

Rhode Island, the "Ocean State," is also home to some of New England's finest beaches, such as Charlestown Breachway State Beach.

what most visitors sought to escape: a ghastly web of commercial development, tacky tourist attractions, and traffic jams. Something had to be done, and quickly, before similarly cheap development overwhelmed the still unsullied Outer Cape.

Help arrived in the person of Senator John F. Kennedy of Massachusetts. Kennedy, whose family vacationed in Hyannis, strongly supported a bill to set aside much of the Outer Cape as a National Park. After three years of careful planning and assuaging of local residents' fears by the National Park Service, John F. Kennedy, now president, signed the Cape Cod bill in 1961, permanently protecting some 27,000 acres and establishing Cape Cod National Seashore. The bill was a landmark in conservation history, not only because the Park Service had successfully contended with some 3,600 privately owned parcels while creating the National Seashore, but Cape Cod was the first park for which Congress approved land-acquisition funds.

One late-summer morning, I'm pondering a mystery, an ancient legend, about the Cape that refuses to die. On a day like this I can believe in almost anything. As Mary and I put our sea kayaks into the flat calm of Cape Cod Bay in Wellfleet, there isn't a breath of wind, and an eerie mist lies over the water.

We point the kayaks at the dunes of Great Island looming on the horizon, and the sharp bows slice the slate gray sea. The sound of the water chuckling along the hull, the brooding fog, and the long, wild shoreline of Great Island all conspire to remind me of the legend of Leif Eriksson and the Vikings, who may have settled here briefly a thousand years ago.

The Norse sagas described a place called Vineland as a land of forests, islands, and lakes remarkable for its abundance of wild grapes. The crude map depicted it as an attenuated peninsula that looks, in fact, very much like Cape Cod, where wild grapes grow in profusion, and where there is no shortage of forests, islands, and lakes.

After an hour of kayaking, we make landfall amid a swarm of horseshoe crabs looking like so many antique bronze helmets strewn across the sand. There's a dead dolphin washed up at the high tide line. We secure the boats, then hike through the dripping pine forest. The soft, sandy trail passes the site of the Great Island Tavern, where 250 years ago whalers and fishermen spent their wages on food, drink, and bawdy female companionship. Today the tavern is gone, swallowed by the forest and the dunes and the tide. But the ghosts are surely here, for it is wilder now than it was then, and this is still a fine place for carousing. Was this Vineland?

We hike out to the very tip of the island at Jeremy Point, where the narrow spit dwindles away to nothing and which will be completely submerged by the tide in a few moments. Like Thoreau, I stand at the edge of America and watch the rising sea flow over my toes, then over my feet. Soon the point is awash, utterly gone. Things have a way of disappearing here, and it's still possible to get lost in the wilds of Cape Cod.

The pure white beaches, crystal clear waters, and extensive underwater sand flats of the Monomoy Islands off the elbow of Cape Cod are more reminiscent of the Bahamas than of New England.

Above
The mighty sea can be a powerful force. A storm pounded the beach and pushed up this six-foot wall of sand.

Left
Storms often deposit flotsam and jetsam high above the tide line in the Cape Cod National Seashore. Here a large piece of driftwood lies among beach grasses where it was tossed by the sea.

Right
A single crab claw lies on the sand where a wave deposited it. Not a person in sight.

Sometimes the ocean is benign . . .

. . . and sometimes it shows an angrier side.

Wispy beach grasses sweep the sand at the edge of the dunes of the Great Beach.

Right, top
Beach roses and beach plums thrive in the dunes along Cape Cod National Seashore.

Right, bottom
A wave rolls onto a long, lonely strand of the Great Beach. Even at the height of summer it is possible to find miles of empty sand on the Outer Cape.

The Pamet River cuts almost entirely across the Outer Cape near Truro.

Beach roses and beach plums also grow in the extensive dunes that stretch behind beaches of Cape Cod Bay.

Above
The Herring River cuts through tidal marshes, dunes, and pitch-pine woodlands in Wellfleet before emptying into Wellfleet Bay.

Left
Gull Pond is one of more than 150 freshwater ponds and lakes that dot the interior of Cape Cod.

The setting sun casts colorful hues in the skies above the Outer Cape's pine woodlands.

A tidal creek meanders through salt marshes and upland pitch-pine forests in Truro.

Above
A footpath through the dunes leads invitingly to the Great Beach and the sea.

Left
A weathered sand fence, meant to control dune migration, stands among beach grasses at Cape Cod National Seashore.

Above
Beach grasses thrive on lower-angle stretches of dunes. Where the dunes are too steep, the sand is bare.

Right
The Great Beach is always evolving. Here, wind and water have eroded a section of dune to reveal a harder layer of sand that is more resistant to erosion.

A gentle wave washes up on the sand.

The sun sets in spectacular fashion over the calm waters of Cape Cod Bay.

Chapter 6

WILD NEW ENGLAND

GEOGRAPHY AND DESTINY

Above
Autumn's rich palette colors a young maple tree
in New Hampshire's White Mountain National
Forest.

Left
The whitewater of the Androscoggin River in
far northern New Hampshire is one of New
England's many popular outdoor-recreation
destinations.

SOMETIMES NEW ENGLAND seems almost mythical—a region steeped in history, the birthplace of American freedom, the cradle of the Revolutionary War. In popular culture, New England is often depicted as a bucolic land of tidy, white-washed churches, of village greens, of sturdy farms with freshly painted barns. Here, according to this portrayal, lives a proud community of self-sufficient farmers and clever craftsmen, of tight-lipped, independent Yankees. There is even a saying attributed to Yankees that goes: "If you want to see how your great-grandparents lived, come to New England."

There is some truth to this picture. In many ways, New England *is* an odd and idiosyncratic place, and New Englanders are an odd and idiosyncratic bunch. Stuck way up in the nation's chilly rafters, far removed from moods and trends of the Heartland, the Sunbelt, and the Bible Belt, New England has a strong sense of identity as a place apart. The region sometimes seems to be fixed in a different time, for the farms and village greens are still quite real; and from Connecticut's Samuel Colt, to Vermont's John Deere, to Massachusetts's Samuel Morse, to today's high-technology pioneers, New Englanders have long valued and fostered cleverness and innovation.

The ascetic streak attributed to Yankees goes back a long way too, for our Puritan forebears were hardly light-hearted folk. In the old days, New Englanders often welcomed strange notions with a good public dunking or a spell in the stocks. If someone really got carried away, the village elders might just have arranged an appointment with the noose or the stake.

A healthy skepticism is still very much a part of the regional character, and many New Englanders still view people from "Away" with a certain amount of suspicion. My home state, Vermont, takes pride in the fact that it chose to remain an independent nation long after the United States declared independence from Britain. The Republic of Vermont joined the United States only in 1791. But even then, founding fathers Ethan and Ira Allen hedged their bets by stashing away an arsenal of twenty thousand muskets and twenty-four cannons, just in case membership in the Union became too confining. To this day, New Hampshire's state motto, stamped on every license plate, remains General John Stark's exhortation to his men at the Battle of Bennington: "Live Free or Die."

Today, to some outsiders, New Englanders can still seem as stern as their cold, northern forests and their craggy, rockbound coast. There is some truth to this as well, for geography is destiny, and in New England the old ways of life are still tied to the landscape.

Nature is in charge here, and wherever you travel in the region you are never far from the outdoors. People live largely according to the rhythms of the four distinct seasons, and many of the primary occupations and recreational activities

Handcrafted wood-canvas canoes are ready for a paddle on Daggett Pond in the Maine Woods.

are directly tied to the land. Whether setting lobster traps, felling pulpwood and timber, hunting deer, gardening, snowshoeing, canoeing, maple sugaring, trout fishing, skiing, farming, snowmobiling, or mushroom and berry picking, New Englanders engage in a rich diversity of traditional, seasonal, landscape-based activities.

The New Englanders' way of working and playing on the land, combined with their distinct sense of cultural and geographical identity, gave birth to a strong heritage of land conservation long before the advent of the modern environmental movement. As early as 1847, George Perkins Marsh, a U.S. congressman from Vermont, called for a conservationist approach to forest management, and he outlined the destructive ecological impacts of deforestation in his seminal book *Man and Nature*. In 1851, Henry David Thoreau declared to the Concord Lyceum that "in wildness is the preservation of the world." A few years later he published his masterpiece on living simply in nature, *Walden*, by some accounts the best-selling book in the history of publishing.

Marsh and Thoreau articulated what many generations of New Englanders before and since have recognized: that the special way of life here is intimately tied to a healthy landscape. New Englanders have long worked hard to preserve the natural surroundings that define their lives, oftentimes using their native cleverness and ingenuity to create new tools—such as multistate, public-private conservation partnerships with organizations such as the Trust for Public Lands—to get the job done.

New England does indeed have treasured National Forests and National Parks, but Yankees are ever distrustful of outside control, and as a result much more of the landscape has been protected through local, state, and regional activity than by federal decree. Almost every village in the region has a town forest and a town conservation commission. Each of the states has many local and regional private conservation land-trusts. In addition, in accordance with long-standing tradition, literally tens of millions of acres of private timberlands in northern New England are managed for multiple use and are open to the public for outdoor activities.

Not only is this homegrown approach to conservation effective, it reflects local values and traditions, and it enjoys wide support all across the social and political spectrum. Though land-use conflicts do arise, acrimony is rare because disputing sides share basic core values. More than any other part of the country, New England is characterized by widespread recognition that the natural landscape, the jobs, and the rural way of life are inseparable. Protect the one, and you protect them all.

New Englanders have long worked to protect their coasts and interior landscapes such as Maine's Mount Desert Island in Acadia National Park.

Above
The ever-shifting sand dunes of the Cape Cod National Seashore house one of the region's most fragile ecosystems.

Right
Striking natural beauty is there to be found throughout the wilds of New England, such as this rushing stream in the Green Mountains.

The sun sets beyond a nameless ridge in Vermont's Green Mountains.

CONSERVATION RESOURCES AND NATURE ORGANIZATIONS

American Farmland Trust
New England Field Office
1 Short Street, Suite 2
Northampton, MA 01060
www.farmland.org

American Rivers
Northeast Field Office
20 Bayberry Road
Glastonbury, CT 06033
www.amrivers.org

The Appalachian Mountain Club
5 Joy Street
Boston, MA 02108
www.outdoors.org

Connecticut River Watershed Council
15 Bank Row
Greenfield, MA 01301
www.ctriver.org

Ducks Unlimited
One Waterfowl Way
Memphis, TN 38120
www.ducks.org

The Nature Conservancy
4245 North Fairfax Drive, Suite 100
Arlington, VA 22203
www.nature.org

Quebec-Labrador Foundation
Atlantic Center for the Environment
55 South Main Street
Ipswich, MA 01938
www.qlf.org

Society for the Protection of
  New Hampshire Forests
54 Portsmouth Street
Concord, NH 03301
www.spnhf.org

Student Conservation Association
689 River Road
PO Box 550
Charlestown, NH 03603
www.sca-inc.org

Trout Unlimited
1300 North 17th Street, Suite 500
Arlington, VA 22209
www.tu.org

Trust for Public Land
New England Regional Office
33 Union Street, 4th Floor
Boston, MA 02108
www.tpl.org

Upper Valley Land Trust
19 Buck Road
Hanover, NH 03755
www.uvlt.org

Vermont Institute of Natural Science
2723 Church Hill Road
Woodstock, VT 05091
www.vinsweb.org

Vermont Land Trust
8 Bailey Avenue
Montpelier, VT 05602
www.vlt.org

SUGGESTED READINGS

Beston, Henry. *The Outermost House*. New York: Penguin Books, 1988.

Cronon, William. *Changes in the Land: Indians, Colonists, and the Ecology of New England*. New York: Hill and Wang, 1983.

Gorman, Stephen. *Northeastern Wilds: Journeys of Discovery in the Northern Forest*. Boston: Appalachian Mountain Club Books, 2002.

Hamlin, Helen. *Nine Mile Bridge: Three Years in the Maine Woods*. Camden, Maine: Downeast Books, 1977.

Huber, J. Parker. *The Wildest Country: A Guide to Thoreau's Maine*. Boston: Appalachian Mountain Club Press, 1981.

Jorgensen, Neil. *A Guide to New England's Landscape*. Chester, Connecticut: Globe Pequot Press, 1977.

Marchand, Peter J. *North Woods: An Inside Look at the Nature of Forests in the Northeast*. Boston: Appalachian Mountain Club Books, 1987.

Marsh, George Perkins. *Man and Nature*. Seattle: University of Washington Press, 2003.

McPhee, John. *The Survival of the Bark Canoe*. New York: Warner Books, 1975.

National Geographic Society. *New England, Land of Scenic Splendor*. Washington, D.C.: National Geographic Society, 1989.

Schneider, Paul. *The Enduring Shore: A History of Cape Cod, Martha's Vineyard, and Nantucket*. New York: Henry Holt and Company, 2000.

Tanner, Ogden. *New England Wilds*. New York: Time-Life Books, 1974.

Thoreau, Henry David. *Cape Cod*. New York: Penguin, 1987.

Thoreau, Henry David. *The Maine Woods*. New York: Penguin, 1988.

Thoreau, Henry David. *Walden*. New York: Random House, 1981.

Waterman, Laura and Guy. *Forest and Crag: A History of Hiking, Trail Blazing, and Adventure in the Northeastern Mountains*. Boston: Appalachian Mountain Club Press, 1989.

Williams, Roger. *A Key into the Language of America*. Detroit: Wayne State University Press, 1973.

INDEX

ABOUT THE AUTHOR

Photograph © Dan Brown

Stephen Gorman's work takes him from the Lewis and Clark Trail in Montana's rugged Missouri Breaks, to remote Inupiat Eskimo villages in arctic Alaska, to the World War II airfields and turquoise lagoons of Midway Atoll. A writer and photographer, he uses his rare combination of skills—writing, photography, and wilderness-travel expertise—to portray the spirit of America's land and people.

Gorman has a lifelong interest in history, conservation, and land-use issues, and his writing and photography benefit from his knowledge of, affection for, and active participation in the subject matter. He holds a master's degree in environmental studies from Yale and a bachelor's degree in American studies from Wesleyan. He worked as a cowboy on a ranch in Wyoming, as an exploration geologist in Alaska and Nevada, and as an Outward Bound wilderness instructor throughout the United States and Canada. Prior to devoting

himself to writing and photography, he also conducted National Wild and Scenic River studies for the National Park Service.

Gorman's previous books include *Northeastern Wilds: Journeys of Discovery in the Northern Forest* (Appalachian Mountain Club, 2002) and *The American Wilderness: Journeys into Distant and Historic Landscapes* (Rizzoli-Universe, 1999). Throughout his career, Gorman has also worked on assignment for national magazines such as *Men's Journal*, National Geographic publications, Discovery Channel publications, *The Boston Globe Magazine*, *Sierra*, *Outside*, and *Yankee*, among others.

He and his wife, Mary, live in Norwich, Vermont, where they enjoy easy access to the mountains, forests, rivers, and lakes of northern New England. You can see more of Gorman's work by visiting his website, www.stephengorman.com.